IMAGES O.

Braintree
and Bocking

IMAGES OF ENGLAND

Braintree and Bocking

John and Sandra Adlam
and
Mark Charlton

NONSUCH

First published 1995
This new pocket edition 2005
Images unchanged from first edition

Nonsuch Publishing Limited
The Mill, Brimscombe Port,
Stroud, Gloucestershire, GL5 2QG
www.nonsuch-publishing.com

British Library Cataloguing in Publication Data.
A catalogue record for this book is available from the British Library.

ISBN 1-84588-182-6

Typesetting and origination by Nonsuch Publishing Limited
Printed in Great Britain by Oaklands Book Services Limited

Contents

Much too busy to write beyond "Braintree agrees with me."

Acknowledgements

The authors are indebted to the following for their contributions to this book:-

Sue Bennett, Ernest Buttle, Daphne & Lez Charlton, Fred Collins,
Keith Collins, Rev. B Davies, Ron Dudman, Lilian Earle, Ken Few,
Melanie Hicks, Una Hitching, Joan & Arthur Hodges,
Derek & Brenda Hutley, Roy Hodson, Neil MacDonald, David McMillan,
Mrs Meesters, Reg Moss, Mrs A Parker, Mr F. Parker, Mr M Parmenter,
Dennis Perry, James Perry, Mike Perry, Joan Scholes, Richard Shackle,
Adam Smith, Connie Smith, Rene Smith, Alex Tanner, Phyllis Thompson, Phyllis
Want, Kate & Colin Wright, and the staff at the Essex Record Office

Introduction

The North Essex town of Braintree and its more residential neighbour, Bocking, have a long and fascinating history rivalling that of any ancient English borough.

Their earliest beginnings can be found in the artefacts of pre-history, when Bronze Age settlers inhabited what is now called Skitts Hill at a time when the area was densely forested. However, the Romans inadvertently laid the foundations for Braintree when they built two military roads, one running east-west from Colchester to St. Albans, the other north-east into the then wastes of East Anglia.

Where these roads crossed marked the location from which Braintree would ultimately develop into its modern form. This happened some seven centuries after the Roman occupation ended when, in 1199, a charter was granted to the town by King John, enabling it to hold a weekly market.

At that time, the majority of the population was centred on the area now known as Chapel Hill, but the charter encouraged a migration towards the old Roman intersection to improve accessibility to the new market.

From the fourteenth century, the woollen cloth trade brought prosperity to Bocking in particular, and the development of bays and says in the sixteenth century ensured the township's continued success in the industry.

Although the trade declined in the latter half of the eighteenth century, its demise heralded the dawn of silk manufacture, and the emergence of nouveau riche mill owners such as the Courtauld dynasty. Today, all that remains of this once-thriving industry is the Working Silk Museum in South Street, Braintree.

The railway age came to Braintree in 1848, and with it the bulk transportation of raw materials. This development encouraged engineering firms such as Crittalls, and Lake and Elliot, to establish themselves in the town. The railway also enhanced the success of the arable and livestock markets.

On to the present, and Braintree has yet to fully recover from the body blow it received in the late 1980s when what might be termed the boom-time-bubble finally burst. While Bocking survives in quiet, residential mode now that the mills are silenced, Braintree's industrial base has changed immeasurably in recent years. Local businesses have had to fight hard to remain competitive.

The town centre too has suffered. If ever a thoroughfare reflected an area's current fortunes, then High Street is the epitome. It has become something of a retail desert, despite now being semi-pedestrianised. The new George Yard was created with the best of visual and economic intentions but has only succeeded in drawing customers away from this historic and attractive highway.

An attempt at greater integration is required while, in the meantime, long-established High Street businesses such as clothiers Townrow's, electrical retailers Nicholls, and jewellers R.G. Swain have demonstrated an admirable capacity to stay afloat in a sea of change. Hopefully their tenacity will be rewarded with a new era of regeneration, not just for this street but for Braintree retailers in general.

People do care, and some signs exist to suggest that more prosperous winds – or zephyrs at least – are beginning to blow.

Manor Street School has continued in its role as an educator by re-opening its doors as a museum, while across the road, the old Town Hall is being used as a tourist information and exhibition centre. At last a *raison d'etre* has been found for the old Post Office, and an exciting new library project is currently under construction, sited between these two Fairfield Road buildings. Further afield, citizens have also seen the demise of the eyesore at the old Fox and Hounds corner, courtesy of builders' merchants Thorogoods, who will transform the site into a garden centre. There is also the promise of a joint rail and bus terminus as part of a plan to regenerate the eastern sector of Braintree, thus giving visitors a more favourable impression of the area. Perhaps things really are starting to look up again for the old town at last.

This book offers a pictorial peep into the past and relies solely on postcard pictures to do so, with the one exception being the photograph of the resplendent Excelsior Band. The postcards are sourced entirely from the private collection of Braintree-based businessman John Adlam, who is more than willing to share them with a wider audience.

Many of the cards come from the early years of the twentieth century. This was a time when this cheap and efficient form of communication was at its peak, when there were three postal deliveries a day, when a letter dispatched at breakfast time would reach its local destination by teatime. This was a time before every household had a telephone.

Despite their humble origins, the postcards that follow provide an absorbing insight into yesteryear Braintree and Bocking, when the century was a lot younger. Also included are chapters on a selection of nearby villages, providing further insight into a bygone era.

This book will hopefully rekindle pleasant memories for those who have lived in the area for any length of time, and be a gentle prompt to the uninitiated that Braintree and Bocking have a history and a heritage of which the inhabitants can be justifiably proud.

One

From the Station
to Market Square

The railway age came to Braintree with the completion of the Maldon–Witham–Braintree line in 1848, at a cost of £14,000 per mile of track. The line crossed the Eastern Counties Railway at Witham, providing a link with London, Colchester and Ipswich. An extension of the track, from Braintree to Bishops Stortford, followed in 1869 but this section was only seeing limited use by 1966, and its official closure followed in 1969. The postcard shows Braintree station with the footbridge for the Bishops Stortford platform.

W. Johnson & Son – merchants dealing in coal, salt, corn, hay and manure – and also cartage agents for the railway's coal depot, which explains the 'G.E.R. Parcels' signwriting on the wagon's canopy. Mr Johnson's business was still going strong into the late 1930s under the name of Johnson and Stratton. This card is postmarked 1914.

South Street looking towards Railway Street. The postcard's correspondent is a soldier named Maurice, and it is addressed to his mother in Greenwich on 11 November 1914, informing her that he is billeted in Cressing Road.

A procession celebrating the Coronation of George V, on 22 June 1911. The three-storey building on the left is Fuller's boot factory and further along, at No. 7, Fairfield Road, are Spooner's Dining Rooms. Mr Spooner was also an antiques dealer. Nearest to the camera, on the right, is the plot of land which at that time would have been due for development in the shape of the silent movie 'Palace' cinema.

'Tonight: "Western Hearts"' proclaims the poster overlooking the cluster of children on the corner of Victoria Street. This postcard is postmarked 1912, the year the Palace was opened. Enlarged in the 1920s in response to competition from the Central cinema in the High Street, the currently disused Embassy replaced the Palace on the same Fairfield Road site in the 1930s.

The old post office and cinema, Fairfield Road. Braintree's main post office was located at 82 High Street until the purpose built Fairfield Road premises were opened in 1931. The post office has since seen fit to move again and is currently based at the Quadrant store along Rayne Road. Plans are afoot to refurbish the Fairfield Road site for use by the Employment Service.

Funded by William Julien Courtauld and designed by Vincent Harris, building work on the Town Hall commenced in 1926. The official opening took place on 22 May 1928. The copper plated frescoes in the Council Chamber depicting the history of Braintree are the work of Maurice Greiffenhagen R.A. The central tower contains a clock with five bells and sitting atop the dome is a bronze figure representing 'Truth', from the Town Arms motto: 'HOLD TO THE TRUTH'. The building is currently in use as a tourist information centre.

A view across Braintree's rooftops taken from the Town Hall Clock tower, c. 1930. Tribble's Saddlery store is to the right of the Bull public house. Across the road next to what is now an estate agents, can be seen Fred Taylor's, Auctioneers, Valuers, Estate and Insurance Agents – and so on!

Same time, same Clock tower, looking eastwards, revealing a view of Manor Street and with the school of the same name enveloped by trees.

Woodfield Road, looking towards the junction with Mount Road. Most of the houses on view on the left-hand side of the road were built between 1895 and 1900, whilst the houses on the right are a little older, 1886-7.

The philanthropist Mr George Courtauld paid for the buildings and ground of Manor Street School, which opened in 1862. This card is postmarked 1910 and in that year Mr Richard W. Davies was the headmaster. The infants' mistress was Miss A. Gray. Manor Street closed its gates as a school in 1990, but fortunately has not been allowed to fall into a state of disrepair, and is currently being put to good use as home to the excellent Braintree District Museum, which celebrated its first year in existence in October 1994.

Manor Street school, early 1920s, with Market Square in the background. The children are flanked by Ernest Quick, headmaster, and Miss Nankivell, school mistress.

Market Square looking toward Manor Street. To the right of Bearman's the bakers is Ludgater's newsagent and postcard publishers, with the office of the Braintree and Bocking Advertiser (established 1859, folded 1920) located over them. At the end of the row is Hutley's, men's outfitters. This family firm ceased trading in February 1995 due to the retirement of Derek and Brenda Hutley. The business was founded by Mr Hutley's grandfather in 1893.

A Market Square view, *c.* 1913 looking towards Fairfield Road. The grand cubed structures on the left marked the entrance to the cattle pens. They made way, in 1928, for the Town Hall. The boards on either side of the entrance to the Crown and Anchor public house are advertising, among other things, Allison's bread, the Palace Cinema, an estate agents, pedal cycles, a furniture shop and a forthcoming fair. To the immediate left of the public house can be seen the shop of B. Rudkin & Son 'Complete House Furnishers'.

Travel back in time by about five years, take several brisk strides beyond the drinking fountain, turn around and we have a view from the lower end of Market Square looking towards Great Square. The drinking fountain, erected in 1882, was yet another bequest by George Courtauld to the people of Braintree.

Market Square, c. 1903. The newly constructed houses in the middle distance mark the location of Victoria Street and the southern boundary of the oblong shaped piece of land once known as the Fair Field. Its other boundaries were Manor Street to the north, Railway Street to the east and Fairfield Road to the west.

Great Square. The Constitutional Club, founded 1893, resided at the location shown here, before moving to the large house at the far end of the Square in 1913, in use as A.A. Spearman's Motors & Cycles shop at the time this picture was taken, in about 1900. The boy nearest the camera, bottom right, is standing by what is currently a travel agents. In previous decades the shop has been home to Van Allen's Fashions, and long before that, Tilcock's Tea and Grocery Provisions. This card, postmarked 1904, is addressed to a Mademoiselle Blaize, residing in Marseilles.

Great Square c. 1935, looking towards High Street. Architectural expert Nikolaus Pevsner is correct in pointing out that the Square is in fact funnel-shaped. Fortunately there is no sign of a pressure group campaigning to change the name to 'Great Funnel'. To the left is F.A. Adams, previously M. T. Adams, stationers. Further along is the overhanging sign of the Bell public house, currently Boots the Opticians. The five-bay white brick building on the right, built in the early 1800s, was demolished in the 1960s.

Two

Bank Street

A view of Bank Street taken from the junction with High Street. The Saracen's Head, currently in use as the Victoria Wine Shop, was once a meeting place for Braintree's 'Four and Twenty'. Further along is the premises of G.T. Bartram O.B.E., J.P., a lifelong servant to the town and a gun and rifle maker who invented several improvements in this field. A man of many interests, he also had a glass and china shop in the same street.

W. & R. Fletcher, butchers, established themselves at No. 52, Bank Street in about 1906, and moved their business to Nos. 10 and 12, Bank Street in the late 1920s.

Spot the difference! These two postcards were printed from the same photograph of Bank Street, taken at the turn of the century; hence they look identical in every respect, until we turn our attention to the prominent display of linen outside Pilcher's Drapery Store and compare it with its sudden disappearance in the lower card. Eye-straining scrutiny of this postcard reveals that someone has applied some skilful artwork to delete the display. This immediately prompts the question: why? Answers on a postcard, please.

Bank Street looking towards the White Hart Hotel and Bocking End. Jenkins the chemist would have been a recent addition to the street's shops at the time this photograph was taken, in about 1910. To the right is the premises of Frederick Pluck, 'Tailors, Hatters, Hosiers and Outfitters'. Jebez Pluck established the business in the 1860's and also had a Witham branch.

Bank Street, looking towards High Street. On view, just beyond the White Hart, is a parade of shops beginning with John Blomfield's Drapery Store, followed by Alden's the Tailors, next along is the National Call Telephone Office and then Taylor's the butchers. Blomfield's shop became the Lloyd's Bank premises before the block was destroyed during an air raid on St. Valentine's Day, 1941. Further down the road, the building with the exposed timberwork was demolished in 1938. This card is postmarked 1905.

A 'Meet' at the White Hart *c*. 1900. The old Co-operative stores can be seen in the background. Alterations were made to this building in January 1875 to make it suitable for trading.

Towards Bocking End from Bank Street *c*. 1911. Mather's stationery, jewellery and postcard publishing shop has recently opened. Trading from the timber framed building are Louisa Cooper, the baker and confectioner, on the left, and to the right, immediately before the clock tower, Elizabeth Pluck, the draper.

Still going Strong
AT
BRAINTREE

Bank Street, outside Barclays Bank, early 1930s. The charabanc belongs to Hutley's, the Coggeshall based carriage firm and no relation to the outfitters of the same name based in Manor Street. Mr Gowers, who used to run the bakery at the top of Notley Road, informs us that he believes the people in the picture to be Co-operative Society employees set for a day trip out, courtesy of the management, at time before paid holiday leave was commonplace.

Three

High Street
and London Road

An early 1920s view of High Street taken from the top floor of what was Fuller's Boot Store. The site is currently occupied by the Midland Bank. To the left of the Westminster Bank, at No. 49, is M. Barnard, 'Florist & Fruiterer', who moved to that location from No. 116 around the time of the Great War. To Barnard's left is Townrow's, followed by the Home and Colonial. The dome, further along, caps the Central Cinema.

An earlier High Street view, with military uniforms on display, assists in approximating the date of this card, as does the seemingly compulsory wearing of caps for the male civilian population! Ludgater's in the Market Square published this card, and must have done a roaring trade in postcards bought by soldiers billeted in the town, who were desperate to keep in touch with loved ones. The pillared building supporting the clock is the Corn Exchange, built in 1839, enlarged in 1877 and demolished in the 1960s.

Right: The Home and Colonial Tea Stores commenced trading at 55 High Street in 1910. Located next door to the International, selling similar wares, competition must have been fierce. Estate agents Roland James currently occupy these premises.

Below: In this 1930 view looking towards Bank Street and Great Square, the derelict and dilapidated premises of the once-thriving Fuller's Boot Store has made way for the new Foster Brothers building. Around the corner, just into Great Square are the sunblinds marking the location of Frank Dance, the tobacconist. Mr Dance began trading at this location in the late 1920s.

High Street, Braintree. 119251

Travelling back to about 1900, we have a view of High Street still firmly entrenched in the Victorian age. The gloriously attired lady is posting a letter at, what was then, the new Post Office, completed in 1896. Fuller's intrusiveness from Bank Street shows why it was possible to get such a good over-view of High Street (shown on page 26).

The International Tea Company Store commenced trading in the town at 57 High Street at the turn of the century, and moved to 58–59 in the early 1930s. The employees in the picture are standing outside the International when it was still at no. 57. This address is currently occupied by Radio Rentals.

High Street looking towards the junction with Bank Street. In the foreground on the right-hand side of the road is Hatfield and Hine's newsagents and postcard publishers. The *Daily Chronicle*'s headline placard reads 'New King's message to His people'. George V succeeded his father Edward VII to the throne in 1910, his coronation was in 1911.

A sombre occasion, 20 May 1910. A funeral procession moves through High Street to mark the death of King Edward VII on 6 May of that year. The picture was taken from a window over what was Ralph Smith's furniture shop, now Glasswell's.

ST. MICHAEL'S CHURCH, BRAINTREE   A/116010

St. Michaels Church, Braintree. 1.

It is generally believed that St. Michael's church has foundations dating from the late twelfth or early thirteenth century, but there have been so many subsequent alterations and additions that the formidable appearance on view today bears little or no resemblance to its original form. Older parts of the church contain Roman bricks and suggestions have arisen from this that the elevated piece of ground on which it is sited may have been a military camp during the Roman occupation. Inside the church, a parchment roll from 1684 lists local folk who perished in the plague of 1665-6.

The fountain at the junction of High Street and St. Michael's Road, with a young boy in bronze holding a fish in one hand and a shell in the other, was designed by John Hodge. It was a gift from William Julien Courtauld to the people of Braintree and was ceremoniously unveiled on 20 July 1937.

St. Michael's vicarage was constructed in the latter half of the 1860s, at a time when architect J.L. Pearson was overseeing restoration work on the church. The vicarage was bought from the church by the Parochial Church Council in 1976, the result of a policy of the diocese at the time to sell off the older buildings in their possession. Now known as Church House, the building is put to good use for various ecclesiastical functions, and deanery, synod and youth group meetings.

The Congregational Church, London Road, built in 1832 at a cost of about £1,400, was born out of a separation from the Bocking End Congregational Church. Now known as Christ Church, the building is shared by worshippers of the United Reformed and Methodist denominations.

London Road with High Street in the distance. The Clare Road junction has yet to be created, which in turn was destined to all but disappear under Pierrefitte Way in 1988. Braintree had a number of oast-houses at this time, and one can be seen in the distance at the rear of the former Wheat Sheaf Hotel, now Flack's.

Taken from just beyond the railway bridge along London Road looking towards Chelmsford c. 1910. It will be a good ten years before the area of land beyond the hedge on the right of this picture becomes the site for the William Julien Courtauld hospital, and a further forty years before the developers pave a route down to Notley Road via Godling's Farm and Giffen's End to create Godling's Way.

The William Julien Courtauld hospital was opened on 16 December 1921, at a personal cost to the generous Mr Courtauld of £20,000. Mrs Courtauld presented an ambulance. The building originally had four wards, and 1938 saw the addition of a maternity ward.

Approaching the brow of the hill of London Road from about 1910. The gates in the
foreground on the left side of the road are long gone and now approximate the entrance to
Acorn Avenue. The villas in the distance currently overlook the William Julien Courtauld
hospital, opened a decade or so after this picture was taken. Run a vertical line up from the
head of the man furthest from the kerb, and the spire of St. Michael's church is just discernible
through the tree branches.

This card, postmarked 1902, shows 'Oaklands', an eye-catching piece of architectural license that once stood proud and remote off London Road, before being demolished to eventually make way for the 'White Courts' estate.

This card was sent on 12 February 1902 from 'Oaklands' to a Miss M.J. Watkins of Ipswich.

Seen through a keyhole in
BRAINTREE

**Just a line from
BRAINTREE**

Four

Rayne Road

Rayne Road looking towards White Hart corner. This is the old Roman highway formerly known as Stane Street. Today, this route continues towards Colchester under the guise of Coggeshall Road. The Methodist chapel was demolished in 1988 to make way for the new George Yard.

Closer to White Hart corner a steam engine in the distance is heading towards the camera. At this time, its role would have been purely functional as opposed to aesthetic. 'English House', also known as 'Twyford House', can be seen on the corner of Panfield Lane. Currently boarded up and formerly used by Eastern Electricity as a showroom, this three storey Georgian mansion reflected the wealth generated by the English family from the 'bay and say' trade.

No road in Braintree can have seen a greater change for the good than Grenville Road. Once a major artery for traffic, including many HGV's making their way through the town, the residents must have breathed a collective sigh of relief when the completion of Pierrefitte Way transformed their road into a quiet cul-de-sac in 1988.

Grenville Road, Braintree.

This picture was taken in about 1908 when there was a timber yard behind the Institute, on the site currently occupied by the DSS Offices. Oliver & Cramp established a timber business further along Panfield Lane, near Currants Farm, in the 1920s.

The Sun Lido was a privately owned concern, located on the site of the 'Essex Barn' formerly the Barn Restaurant, Rayne Road. The Lido has long since closed, but in its heyday boasted one of the finest swimming pools in Essex.

Five

Coggeshall Road

White Hart Hotel, Braintree

The White Hart Hotel dates from the late sixteenth century and is located at the point where Braintree becomes Bocking. It sits at the crossroads where the Roman Stane Street, running east to west, is intersected by a lesser military road heading north east from Chelmsford. The eighteenth century saw the inn become a coaching house and with it came major alterations which widened the original building, creating the kink in the road that has still to be negotiated by drivers as they enter Coggeshall Road from Rayne Road. The White Hart is one of many inns which once lined Braintree and Bocking's main thoroughfares, offering food, drink and rest for pilgrims and journeymen.

Leonard J. Alden established himself in Coggeshall Road at the turn of the century. By 1905 he also had premises just around the corner in Bank Street, which, in subsequent years, became his sole outlet. This picture of the Coggeshall Road shop was taken in about 1906 and is currently occupied by Pyramid Fabrics and Rob's Tackle.

This was Mr Alden's private residence, 'Erceldoune', in Coggeshall Road. The card, postmarked 1920, is addressed to a Miss Alden in London and is signed 'Mother'.

This card, postmarked 1915, shows Coggeshall Road beyond the White Hart junction looking towards what is still known, by some locals, as the Fox & Hounds corner. The building to the left is the County Court, built in 1852 at a cost of £3,000. It is currently in use as the local public library. In March, 1995 building work began on Braintree's new library, on the site between the old Town Hall and the former Post Office. The plans for the £2.2 million scheme give every indication that the finished result will be a design that is innovative and eye-catching. *Opposite above*: Continuing along the same road to the 'Fox & Hounds' corner, in about 1910, Crittall's manufacturers and worldwide distributors of metal window frames, have yet to build their main offices at a stone's throw beyond the junction. The corner where the public house

was located has been an eyesore and a poor advertisement for the town for many years, and it is to everyone's benefit that Thorogoods, the builders merchants located in Upper Railway Street, have purchased this site and have it earmarked for redevelopment as a garden centre that will take in the derelict terraced houses around the corner in Coggeshall Road as well.

Opposite below: Courtauld Road looking towards Bradford Street, with further down the road on the left, the entrance to Bocking Place. In A History of Bocking, compiled by members of the Women's Institute, there is an interesting account of this road's predecessor: 'The new Courtauld Road replaced the old Dead Lane. This was the burying place for the victims of the Plague'. If it were still visible, its route would take it from the same starting point as Courtauld Road, along Coggeshall Road before gently peeling off to make its way through the grounds of Bocking Place. Further along it would pass within yards of the north facing wall of the Masonic Lodge before meeting with the Causeway.

COGGESHALL ROAD, BRAINTREE

Courtauld Road, Bocking.

Jubliee Oak Corner looking towards Braintree c. 1910. The oak was planted in commemoration of Queen Victoria's Diamond Jubilee of 1897. Directly behind the tree is the King's Head public house, identified by the large oblong 'Ridleys' sign positioned over the entrance. Further along the road towards Braintree, just beyond the houses at the far end in this picture, is the entrance to what was then Manor Road, now known as East Street.

Cressing Road looking towards Coggeshall Road, c. 1914. The workmen on view can be seen tarring and rolling the pavement. The bay-windowed houses were built in 1903, the Coronation Cottages on the right are a little older, 1897. Those nearest the camera would have overlooked the old isolation hospital, which has subsequently made way for St. Paul's church and the Woodlands complex.

Further along Cressing Road at around the same time. The houses on the left, from as far back as the top of Chapel Hill, overlooked a large area of allotment gardens. The large weavers' cottage on the right originally had three two-up, two-down dwellings under its single thatched roof before being converted into one property in the 1950s. Next along is a terrace built in 1897 and immediately beyond them is the Jubilee Oak stationed at the junction with Coggeshall Road.

Six

Bocking End
to Bradford Street

Brocking End, Braintree.

The Braintree and West Essex Co-operative Society Ltd – which mercifully saw its new Bocking End premises trading under the comparatively abbreviated title of The Society's Central Stores – officially opened its doors to the public on 31 August 1907. The building had more to offer than just catering for the departmental trade. The first floor had a hall designed to accommodate 300 people for parties, wedding receptions, dances and exhibitions. This impressive building also had reading and committee rooms and was sadly demolished, along with its clock turret, in 1972. Just beyond the stores can be seen the gate pillars that once marked the entrance to the Institute.

Opposite above: One source suggests that the 'Causeway' gets its name from the severity of the kerb and the subsequent erection of the magnificent iron railings to protect the unwary from a potentially nasty fall. They were removed in the 1940s as a contribution to the war effort, although this was little more than a propaganda exercise, as the metal was useless for recycling. The building behind the Congregational Church's tombstones is 'Bocking British School', which, lacking status as a listed building, was demolished in 1979 to make way for Braintree District Council's 'Causeway House'. The 'bobby' in the picture appears to be devoid of the problems facing his contemporary counterparts. It would be nice to imagine him upholding law and order by cheerily administering a clip round the ear to a cheeky chappie who would learn his lesson and know his place. Move along now...

Opposite below: The Public Gardens, situated just off the Causeway, cover 5½ acres and were donated to the people of Braintree and Bocking by Sydney Courtauld, who, along with his wife Sarah Lucy, formally opened the grounds on 26 November 1888.

1444   Bradford Street, H...

WINTER SCENE: ENTRANCE. BRAINTREE & BOCKING PUBLIC GARDENS.

RAY STUDIOS, LTₒ
BRAINTREE.

The correspondence on the reverse of this postcard, addressed to a friend in Brixton, is written by a woman who was present in the Public Gardens when this photograph was taken. Unfortunately, she stops short at claiming to be the elegant lady coyly looking towards the camera in this idyllic scene. Using a curiously evasive style of prose, she writes: 'This was taken when I was sitting in the Gardens, but they told me I should not be in it. Although you cannot see my face, it is meant for me'. The card is postmarked 16 December 1909, and the picture was taken during the summer of that year.

The thatched bandstand is still present, and continues to maintain a long established tradition of playing host to local bands, giving enjoyable summer concerts. A more recent fixture in the grounds is the Knot Garden, created in 1986 as a permanent memorial to John Ray, the celebrated local botanist. This card is postmarked 1902.

Just beyond the Public Gardens, the junction with Courtauld Road (known as New Road at the time the above picture was taken, before the Courtaulds lent their name to it) sees the end of the Causeway and the start of Bradford Street, which for centuries has been a major artery instrumental in merging Braintree and Bocking. For certain periods in history the street, which once had a high number of inns and hostels, has generated considerable wealth by catering for weary pilgrims in search of a place to eat, drink, and perhaps, even sleep, before continuing on their journey to holy shrines in Suffolk and Norfolk.

GREAT SQUARE, BRAINTREE.

Further along Bradford Street, we stop just before the King's Head, c. 1912. Mark Barns was the landlord of this public house for several years up until the Great War. Across the road is Bearman's the baker and Walford's the seed merchant. Further down the same side of the street are excellent examples of architectural design, some dating from as far back as the thirteenth century, that have justifiably accorded the street status as an area of great historical importance. In the middle of the road on his horse and cart, is Mr Johnson (see page 10) going about his business.

Bradford Street, Bocking.

'This little piggy went to market' or in this case the prime pieces of pork being shepherded along Bradford Street – not an advisable practise in the interminable traffic of the 1990s – have probably just made the journey from Market Square. There was no shortage of butchers in the Street at the time this picture was taken in about 1912. They included Mr Benham, Mr Perry and Mr Phillips, all of whom would have welcomed the unsuspecting sight trotting towards them!

The Six Bells Corner, Bocking

Approaching 'Six Bells Corner', c. 1900. The row of cottages on the left stands, it is believed, on the site of the ancient chapel of St. James. The bay window by the end wall marks the location of the sub-Post Office, at this time run by Mrs Emily Willis. The carriageway leads to the Bocking Brewery. The overhanging sign highlights the old Six Bells' close proximity to the road. It was demolished in the 1930s and a new public house with the same name was built, this time located well away from the corner. The woman and children are outside 'Tudor House' (built in about 1520) at a time before contemporary trends decreed that the timberwork should be exposed.

A few paces beyond the old Six Bells, we arrive at the junction with Church Lane. The billowing trees overhanging the wall are in Boleyn's Park, destined for development in the form of the Braintree College of Further Education. To the right, just beyond Tudor House, is the forge of Frederick Waters, blacksmith. William Waters founded the business in the late 1850s and the family name continued plying their noble trade here into the 1920s.

Bocking Bridge is located over the river Blackwater at the point where Bradford Street and Broad Road meet. It replaced the old wooden Bradford Bridge in 1927. The turreted building is the Catholic Church of St. Francis and the Immaculate Conception, built in 1898-9.

A view from the other side of the bridge, looking back towards Bradford Street. On the right by the Blackwater is Cane's Mill, the sixteenth-century fulling mill, which is also known to a lesser extent as Bradford Mill. The sign pointing the way to the St. Francis Convent School is located at the entrance to Convent Lane, which also led to the now demolished Hobbs or Straits Mill.

St. Francis' Orphanage with the church still in view further down the road. The convent also included a school building. The orphanage building has since been extended and is now in use as a nursing home for the elderly.

A morbid subject for a postcard – a cemetery! Is such a card sent to one's friends, or enemies?

Seven

Church Lane
and on to Bocking

54171. BRAINTREE CHURCH ROAD, BOCKING

Left: Church Lane with the junction with Bradford Street in the distance. Coldnailhurst Avenue has yet to cut into Queen's Head Meadow on the right and make its way westward towards Panfield Lane. The lady with the perambulator is situated at the future entrance to the new road.

Below: Church Lane, *c.* 1914. This picture was taken from almost the same spot as the previous one, across the road from what is now the goods entrance to Braintree College, but this time the camera is looking towards Deanery Corner. 'Boleyns' is to the right, behind the iron gate. The stable yard lies beyond, obscured by the trees in this picture.

CHURCH LANE. BOCKING.

W.E.E.R.

Hill Villas, five pairs of houses situated at the top of Polly's Hill, Church Lane, just beyond Resting Seat House.

The wooden bridge at Bocking, shortly before work commenced on the new brick Kings' Bridge. For this picture, the cameraman would have been standing with his back to the old Courtauld mill. The horse stops briefly for a profile shot before continuing its journey towards Braintree. Beyond the bridge, to the right, is the area of undeveloped land known, at this time, as Bridge End Place.

Kings' Bridge looking towards Deanery Corner. The bridge was named in commemoration of the reign of Edward VII and the Coronation of George V. Completed in 1914, it replaced the ageing wooden bridge. This picture was taken from King's Corner, but, unlike the bridge, there is no connection with any royal personage here. The corner is named after Christopher King, a seventeenth-century clothier.

There are four structures of great architectural, historical and spiritual interest in this picture. To the left, at the top of Bovington Road, is the Royal Oak public house overlooked by the Courtauld silk factory. The iron fence surrounds the Workmen's Hall, built in 1884 for the benefit of the factory employees. St. Mary's church, to the right, was originally founded in the eleventh century, but most of what is on view now is of fifteenth- and sixteenth-century origin. This card is postmarked 1913.

By the year 2000, the Royal Almshouses, seen here just beyond the Workmen's Hall, had provided 560 years of shelter to Bocking folk. Rebuilt in 1869, the Church Street dwelling was originally set up in 1440 to house about a dozen of the local poor, with a deed arranged by landowners, John Doreward, who was granted an endowment for the project by King Henry VI. The card is postmarked 1903.

CAUTAULD'S SILK FACTORY, BOCKING.

A view of what was known collectively as the 'Steam Factory', from a card postmarked 1909. Samuel Courtauld purchased the baize mill, on the left, from clothier John Savill in 1819. The new silk mill is on the right. These historic buildings no longer exist, the former having been demolished in 1920, the latter in 1987–8. However, a much more favourable fate has befallen the lodge keeper's house, the white building in the picture. It was dismantled, brick by brick, in the 1920s and re-erected at High Garrett as a private residence.

Church Street, Bocking, c. 1900. The success of the Braintree and West Essex Co-operative Society Ltd. encouraged the decision to open a branch premises in Church Street. The shop opened on 23 January 1874, in the form of a cramped double-fronted cottage. By 1879, larger premises were being sought and the freehold property, shown in this picture, was purchased by the Society and ready for trading by late 1880.

Church Street, Bocking looking west towards the bridge over the Pant tributary. The Co-operative Society's new branch store, which opened in 1913, dominates the picture. Further down the street is the sign for the 'Black Boy' Inn.

The 'Black Boy' Inn, Church Street, has foundations dating from as long ago as 1634. From the late 1890s until just before the Great War, Bocking's fire-fighting service, which initially comprised one superintendent and four men, kept the fire engine at the inn yard. In 1984, the pub was re-named the 'Retreat'.

Church Street looking towards the River Pant. The house nearest to the camera on the right is currently in use as a ladies' hairdresser. The fence and hedge overlooked by the end wall have since made way for a newsagents, 'The Paper Shop'. The proprietor, Mr Parmenter, informs us that the building opened its doors for business, initially as a Post Office, in 1938. The water pump that served this end of the Street can be seen to the left of the telegraph pole.

A view of Church Street taken adjacent to what is currently a fish and chip shop. The houses on both sides of the street in this picture are still standing; their present appearance show that they are well maintained by their owners. The correspondence on the reverse of this card, signed 'Annie' and addressed to a Miss Goss of Stratford, explains the 'X' in the picture. This is where Annie was staying, 'opposite Green Lane' she writes. Although it may have been known as such at the time she posted this card (19 August 1913), it is currently known as Fennes Road.

Bocking Church Street, c. 1900 looking towards the 'Four Releet' junction. The wooden barrier, nearest to the camera on the left, leads to the Bull public house. This, along with the Tabor tied cottages further up the road and the thatched house at the far end, no longer exists. Mr James Perry, of Perry and Sargent Ltd., Builders, informs us that the semi-detached stone cottages with '1821' on the side wall were dismantled by his father, Thomas George Perry, in 1962 to make way for a retirement bungalow further back from the road. However, he retained several feet of the front and side outer walls of the old cottage and utilized them as a ready-made stone wall, shielding the new bungalow from the road and adjacent properties.

People skating and generally having fun on the flooded, frozen area of meadowland by the river Blackwater, February 1912. In the distance is Hobbs or Straits Mill, now demolished. The lady who wrote the correspondence on the reverse of this card is actually in the picture. She signs herself as Dot and has, conveniently, placed ticks above her head and the man to her left, whom she names as Ernie. This area is now part of the Great Bradfords Estate.

I am thinking of you
. . at . .
BRAINTREE

*After the postman has
knocked at your door
And this little
    post card you see :
You'll know that whoever
    forgets you to-day,
That you are
    remembered by me.*

I shall "Whelk-ome" you at

BRAINTREE

Eight

Work, Rest and Play

Built in about 1888, this grand Courtauld family residence, known as Bocking Place, opened its doors as the Braintree Intermediate School in 1922. It closed in 1938, the result of a merger with the County High School along Coggeshall Road.

On the night of Thursday, 9 December, 1909, a fire broke out in the spinning room on the second floor of Courtauld's Braintree mill at Chapel Hill. By next morning the building, completed just six years before, lay in ruins. Work on a new spinning and winding mill quickly commenced and was in operation, and making a profit, within a year of the fire.

The Braintree Local Board of Health was founded in 1850 as a result of the Public Health Act. The Board's responsibilities included the management of the town's sanitation, lighting and pavement maintenance. The early fire service, then based in Coggeshall Road, also came under the BLBH's jurisdiction, thus explaining the signwriting, partly concealed by the fine body of pioneering firemen, on the side of the wagon. In full it reads: 'Braintree Local Board'. This card is postmarked 1907.

The Excelsior Band and the Braintree Town Mission Band entertained local folk in the early years of the century. They came into their own as morale boosters during the Great War.

A polite letter of acknowledgement from 1922 to a customer satisfied with service received from the family firm, has an extensive letterhead which reads: 'Joscelyne's Motor Removal Service for Household Removals, Eastern Counties and London and All Parts'. At this time, Joscelyne's head office was based in the High Street (Telephone No. 25) with depositories in New Street and Fairfield Road. The firm also had offices at Colchester and Bishop's Stortford.

Lovers Lane – thought to have been near the Courtauld Factory at Mill Hill – will probably rekindle the memories of some of the inhabitants of Braintree!

Nine

Notley Road and through Black Notley, White Notley and Faulkbourne

Coronation Avenue suffered four fatalities and damage to virtually every house during a Zeppelin raid in April 1916. This card is postmarked August 1927.

The road to Black Notley viewed from Hoppit Bridge c. 1910. At that time this part of Notley Road was susceptible to flooding, but modern engineering has virtually eliminated the problem.

The Norman church of St. Peter and St. Paul was much restored in 1879 by A.W. Blomfield and can seat approximately 120 people. It has a carved oak south porch and a shingled belfry containing five bells, which were re-hung in 1950. John Ray (1627–1705) is buried in the adjoining churchyard.

John Ray, the naturalist, was born in this cottage on 27 November 1627, the third child of the village blacksmith, Roger Ray and his wife, Elizabeth, who was a herbs-woman. In 1986 a bronze statue of John Ray was unveiled in Bank Street, Braintree.

An idyllic view of the road to Witham taken in 1905, with the Vine public house in the foreground. The slightly lower end of the building contained a shop which was run by the landlords, who at this time were the Richardsons, and has been dated c. 1640.

Eight years later, in February 1913, the Vine was badly damaged by fire. The licensee at this time was Wilfrid G. Sandford, who was "Licensed to sell beer by retail to be drunk on the premises". Another minor disaster occurred on 24 August 1944, and Mr Howlett, landlord, claimed for "commodities damaged by enemy action".

Black Notley Mill stood next to the Reindeer public house and was run by water and then turbine. Seen in this 1930s view, it was already falling into disrepair, and was demolished just before the Second World War, the villagers using the wood for their fires. The barns standing at right angles to the road have long since disappeared and were used for horses, pigs, cows and grain storage, and had the village tap on the wall facing the road.

In August 1933 a soldier billeted in Black Notley sent this view of the mill pond to his wife in Married Families Hospital near Folkestone, following the birth of their daughter.

The mill pond which, following the demolition of the mill, was eventually drained and a house built on the site.

Black Notley

78995.

The thatched cottage in the foreground of this 1920s/30s view of The Street was the home of Mr Ardley, a roadman, and his daughter, Lucy.

The bold sign advertising "Teas" marks the site of the bakery (the last baker being Mr Tabner) and tea-room. The latter was a favourite with the off-duty nurses from the hospital. The small building on the left, partially hidden by bushes, is the Notley Baptist Fellowship hall where, during the 1940s and 50s, Mr Heddles, a tallyman from Witham, conducted a Sunday School.

Lord Lambourne laid the foundation stone for the King Edward VII Memorial Hall which stands at the top of the drive to the Black Notley Sanatorium. The hall was presented to the hospital by the King Edward VII Association for the prevention of consumption, then tuberculosis in Essex, on 3 August 1928. Concerts, dances and film shows were some of the activities put on in the hall for the patients. It is now home to the Pines Day Nursery.

Black Notley Sanatorium was built in 1905 for 20 smallpox patients. Male and female consumptive cases followed in 1913, and in 1929 it grew to 188 beds when tuberculosis patients were admitted, and included a maternity unit for expectant mothers with tuberculosis. Shown here are the administration block and South Pavilion.

The hospital originally had three hut verandahs, which enabled the tubercular patients to be put into the fresh air while still confined to their beds. During the Second World War a military hospital was added and was run by the Emergency Medical Services. At one time, a cloth hung in the Administration Block which the soldiers in the hospital had embroidered with their names and regiments.

Bulford Mill was a corn and fulling mill on the River Brain in the early 1700s, and it is recorded that in 1707 the cost of a pair of millstones, including £1 for cartage, was £12 10s. (£12.50). Joseph Savill purchased the mill in 1804 as part of his effort to carry on the wool trade in Essex, but being unable to do so, the mill passed into the ownership of Richard Dixon and used for corn milling. The last miller was Francis Blyth, who produced flour from 1914 until 1947. The mill had become five storeys by the end of the nineteenth century, and although now converted for living accommodation, looks much as it did when Blyth left.

The first six houses on the left of the road from Braintree into White Notley were built by G Collins, builder, in about 1929; the next eight having been built ten years perviously.

White Notley Station on the Braintree to Witham line, seen here on a card postmarked 1908. The station house still exists, but the signal-box has been removed.

Station Road looking towards the station. To the right of the railings is a ford which was, and probably still is, popular with the village children, who spent long hot summer days picnicking, paddling and fishing.

At the centre of the village stands the fourteenth century Cross Keys public house, which at one time was Chappell's Brewery. The village tap was sited by the fence to the left and just beyond the Cross Keys can be seen a small building with a curved roof, dated 1828, which was the village lock-up. After falling into disrepair, the lock-up was eventually removed in the early 1980s and replaced by a bench seat.

Post Office, White Notley.

In the early 1900s the Post Office and stores was run by George Harrington, then Mrs Clara Harrington (George's wife?), and finally by Edmund Ibbett, who appears to have given up the Post Office side of the business in 1911/12, when it moved to its present location opposite the Cross Keys public house. The ownership of the stores changed again in the mid-1930s to Harry Ibbett, who was probably Edmund's son. He was also a tallyman, using a horse and cart for his rounds, and a watch repairer, and used the village lock-up as a store-house for his goods.

The little girl in Church Hill is standing outside the house belonging then to Granny Collins. She was grandmother to the family of G Collins, builder, and later, undertaker. Their first funeral was that of Mr Borrett, landlord of the Cross Keys public house, sometime between 1929-33.

The small gate into the grounds of White Notley Hall was known as the "suicide gate", although why is a mystery. One former inhabitant of the village thought it might have referred to the difficulty one might have trying to negotiate the path through the gate following a visit to the adjacent Cross Keys public house!

The central timber-framed part of the hall was built in about 1530, with a brick wing added around 1580. The Hall belonged to the Brewster family for two centuries. Unoccupied between 1912 and 1914, it was bought by Colonel Reid-Scott, who was in charge of the White Notley Home Guard. In the grounds is a lake, at the east end of which once stood a water mill.

The earliest mention of the church dedicated to St. Ethelreda is in 998 A.D. and the font dates from 1400. The village was originally thought to have been sited in the field opposite the church, where Roman remains have been found, and an archway in the church is built of Roman bricks. This card was sent to East Ham, London, in August 1938, and the sender writes "The heat was unbearable on Sunday".

Whilst vicar at White Notley from 1851 to 1857, the Reverend Bennett commenced building the school in the vicarage garden. It was re-designed in 1894 with the addition of a classroom, making it T-shaped, after the government decreed that children aged 3 to 7 and 8 to 14 should be separated. In 1910 the leaded light windows (still in evidence in this 1906 view) were removed, with the exception of the two dormers, following an inspection report that declared that they did not admit enough light. The latest major alterations were in 1994, incorporating the original building and built in a sympathetic style. The average attendance in 1894 was 78; in 1950 it dropped to 60, and now stands at 101.

White Notley Vicarage, where during the benevolent Reverend Bennett's ministry, he had the village school built in the grounds in the 1850s.

Mr & Mrs Gunner lived in "Roselea" when this card was posted in January 1911. The house still looks much the same, apart from the front door having been replaced by a window, and the removal of the hedge, fence and gate.

In the mid-1800s, the building on the left, among the trees, was the poorhouse, which at one time housed four families. Today it is divided into two cottages. In the distance, beyond the car, can be seen barns that belong to Oak Farm.

At the time of this postcard, c. 1930, the village was owned by the Parker family who lived at Faulkbourne Hall, and housed their employees. The outer two of the terrace of four houses were built in 1909, while the inner two are considerably older. The elegant chimneys no longer exist, and the thatched roof was replaced with tiles in the 1940s. The old letter box indicated, was at a height convenient for transferring the mail from the Post Office straight to the driver of the mail coach. The inhabitants of Pump Cottage, (far right) which was pulled down in the early 1950s, used to be able to tell which of the villagers was drawing water, by the action of the pump handle.

FAULKBOURNE.

6400

The North Lodge, shown on this card postmarked 1916, is at one entrance to Faulkbourne Hall. During the Second World War a large searchlight was sited in an adjacent field.

FAULKBOURNE HALL 1679.

Faulbourne Hall is an early fifteenth-century timber-framed house, with brick additions from 1439, and is thought to be built on the site of a Roman villa. The brick tower was added in the second half of the fifteenth century and has a staircase built entirely of brick, including a solid moulded handrail. Bought by Sir Edward Bullock in 1637, it was then home to seven generations of the family, and was John Ray's home from 1677 to 1679.

Fred Spalding
Photo.
Chelmsford
Copyright

The South Lodge, along with its partner at the opposite end of the drive, is thought to have been built in the mid-1800s.

Although there is mention of a "Parsonage House" in Faulkbourne in a survey carried out in 1610, the Rectory seen here was built during the 1840s for Walter Trevelyan Bullock, Rector of Faulkbourne, by his father, Jonathan Bullock. Colonel John Parker purchased the house in 1944 and lived there until his death in 1979. The present owners have re-named the property "Carbonells".

Ten

Rayne

The Swan Inn, seventeenth-century with later additions, was once kept by a Mr Swan. Overseers of the poor met here and the post was brought here before the opening of an official post office in Rayne. The cottage on the corner opposite the Swan, which has since been demolished, housed a sweet shop, and also sold rice pudding so thick that it was bought by the slice for an old penny.

Rayne House, built in 1771 by Mr John English, a Braintree wool merchant, with large cellars to store 'Bocking' – a white wool cloth made in the area. The ground floor has a Regency glazed iron verandah with a curved glass roof. The large pond was part of the Rayne House property, and had a bridge to an island and a small boat. The surrounding garden was beautifully kept and stocked with flowers and shrubs.

Seventeenth-century 'Turners' in Stane Street was altered extensively in the eighteenth and nineteenth centuries. The house was sold for £100 in 1616, to Simon and Ann Bridge of Felsted, whose son, John, founded a school three miles from Boston, Massachusetts, which became Harvard University.

Medley House, an eighteenth-century timber-faced house. The yard of the east wing, 'Pennells', was used for some years as a cooper's business.

Thomas Hawkes came from Marylebone, London in 1867 and lived and worked in Rayne until his death in 1904, when his son, W.E. Hawkes, took over the running of the Post Office and Stores (ably assisted by Harold and Dickie Richardson – pictured above) until he retired in 1933. The building has been used for a variety of business ventures since then including antiques, 'The Cauldron' restaurant, and is currently an Indian restaurant.

The ivy-clad house on the far right is 'The Laurels', built in 1856, home of Mr Peene of Rayne Foundry, who came to Rayne after leaving Heybridge in 1855. At the far end of the buildings on the left, is a listed building which was the village wash-house.

'The Cock' public house was not longer licensed by 1790, but it re-opened some time in the nineteenth century.

The field opposite the Swan is now home to the village hall, having been moved here in 1954 from Brocks Meadow. It was replaced by the present one which commenced building in 1974.

The Brock family, farmers, builders and undertakers, traded from premises which consisted of a house, workshops, and outhouses built by John Brock, at the bridge end of New Street. Following the death of John Brock in 1915, the business was run by his sons, William and Leonard. The building side of the company ceased in 1953 with the death of William, and trading ceased completely in 1967 when Leonard, who lived in the house nearest the camera, died.

The first train through Rayne Street left Braintree on 26 February 1869 bound for Bishops Stortford. A single track, it was used to transport farm produce and products from Rayne Foundry, as well as passengers. Around 1900, the signal box had a phonograph and thus became a popular meeting place for the young men of Rayne. Trade and passenger use dwindled after the First World War, but during the Second World War it became busy again, particularly for American servicemen. Passenger service ceased in 1952 and the station closed finally in 1964.

Mr Harry Goodey, Coal Merchant (born in 1875 in Sudbury, Suffolk, and died in 1955) traded from his coal yard by Rayne Station, from approximately 1915 until just before the Second World War. Before using the magnificent vehicle pictured above, he made his deliveries by horse and cart. He was also known for taking racing bets and being a lover of whist.

After the closure of the school at the Maltings (for the poorer parishioners) and the Dame School at Tudor Cottage in the Gore, the Felsted & Rayne United District School, complete with headmaster's house, opened in 1878 for 210 children. This in turn closed when the new Rayne County Primary School opened in 1975. The lady pictured in the school grounds is Miss Hicks, a third year teacher who lived in Braintree.

Third year pupils and teachers in 1909.

RAYNE   WAR. MEMORIAL

Erected on Rayne Hall Green and dedicated to those who lost their lives in the First World
War, it now has an additional plaque for those who gave their lives in the Second World War.

2622. COTTAGES AT RAYNE.

These thatched cottages situated near Rayne Hall Green and known as 'Highways', have altered little over the intervening years since they were built.

Mary's Cottage, built in the eighteenth century (pictured on the left of this postcard) was named after Mary Saville who died in 1949. The Saville family had the tenancy for 200 years and several of them were parish constables. At the rear of the cottage is the lock-up, which was built in 1819, and was used to keep occupants overnight to sober up, or before being taken to Braintree police station.

Eleven

High Garrett

High Garrett looking towards Halstead. The road to Gosfield lies to the left and to Bocking to the right. Presiding over the junction in sleepier times, before it was swamped by motor cars, is Rose Cottage, which is still there today.

High Garrett junction looking from the Halstead direction. Foley House sits beyond the brick wall, on the road to Bocking. Foley Lodge is to the right, at the start of Gosfield Road.

Closer to the junction, this colour tinted card from 1905 shows 'Folley House' as it was known then. Completed in 1885, it replaced Samuel Courtauld's old 'Folly House'. The current derivation of the original name is 'Foley House'. Recent years have seen the building in use as a Barnardo home and as a restaurant. It is now a home for the profoundly deaf.

Construction work on the Unitarian Chapel and school-room began in the 1850s. It was funded by Samuel Courtauld, who owned most of High Garrett at this time. The building is currently home to a wholesale florist business.

A mid-1920s view of Green Lane, now know as Sunnyfields Road, looking towards the main road through High Garrett.

This view of the main road through High Garrett, looking towards the Gosfield/Halstead junction, was taken in about 1918. The picture book cottage is still there, and continues to show off its thatched roof. The casual chaps looking into the camera would be ill-advised to pose for such a shot on this busy road today.

Twelve

Cressing

Cressing Temple – home to the Knights Templar after being granted Cressing in 1137 by Queen Matilda. In 1314, following the Papal Bull of Pope Clement V, the lands passed into the hands of the Knights Hospitallers, until the land was confiscated by Henry VIII in 1540. The Barley Barn (left), c. 1200 is an aisled structure, 120ft (36.6 metres) long by 48ft (14.6 metres) wide,

and was much altered in the sixteenth century, and the porch added in the late seventeenth century. The Wheat Barn, c. 1260 is 130ft (31.6 metres) long by 44ft (13.4 metres) wide, and has not been altered as much as its companion. It is amazing to realise that each barn was probably built in a single season, between the end of March and the beginning of November.

Church End in the early 1900s. The gentleman pictured above is standing outside the Horseshoes public house, now a private residence, and could well be Arthur Pease who was the publican at this time. The building on the extreme right housed the village smithy. The houses on the left were demolished in the 1950s.

Built in about 1600, this view was taken in the 1930s.

All Saints' church was probably built in the twelfth century, although earlier foundations have been found, and was restored in the early nineteenth century. In the chancel is a monument to Anne, wife of Henry Smith of Cressing Temple, 1907. The religious of the village were well catered for; in addition to the church, there were two chapels belonging to the 'Peculiar People' and a Mission Hall.

At the time this card was posted, the vicar of Cressing was Jabez William Padbury (1910–1916) and probably shows him posing for this photograph at the side of the vicarage, which is now a private house as Cressing no longer has a vicar resident in the village. The vicarage was the birthplace of Field Marshall Sir Evelyn Wood VC in 1838.

The Street in about 1920 showing, on the right and jutting out from the row of cottages, the workshop belonging to Brown the carpenter.

The Street, Cressing.

To the extreme left of this card from about 1930 is one of the two chapels belonging to the 'Peculiar People'; while in the distance, at the bend in the road, is the 'Ashes' public house, c. 1678.

The van parked outside the 'Ashes' in this postcard c. 1930, belonged to Sibley the Baker.
Further down the road, the last building on the left was formerly the 'Red Lion' public house,
which 150 years ago is reputed to have been raided by the 'Coggeshall Gang'.

Hawbush Green in the early 1900s – the thatched cottage was the bakehouse and home of Mr
Collins and later his step-son, Mr Lambert. Next to this is the second chapel belonging to the
'Peculiar People', with beyond this some of the first council houses to be built in Cressing.

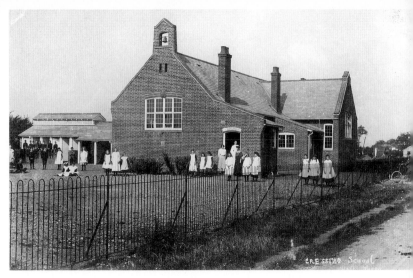

Cressing School 1905, was built in 1901, and remains much the same except for the addition of portable classrooms and an extension to the left.

Originally Bulford Station, it was re-named Cressing Station (seen here in the 1960s) following an incident in 1911 when a London clerk misdirected an army contingent, complete with full equipment and baggage, to Essex instead of Wiltshire.

Thirteen

Stisted

Standing on the site of a mill possibly belonging to the monks of Canterbury Cathedral in 1086, Stisted Mill looks much the same as it would have done in 1775, when it ran a pair of fulling stocks and ground corn. During the nineteenth century, when the area flooded and the water wheel could not be used, a steam engine worked another pair of stones at the opposite side of the mill. The water wheel was turning the stones until the end of the First World War, and the sack hoist until 1960.

The South Lodge once stood at the entrance to Stisted Hall, near the entrance to Braintree Golf Club. The still existing North Lodge was, for 57 years, the home of Lilian Earle, whose father-in-law was the publican of the Onley Arms, and who wrote *Clover Hay – A Personal Portrait of Stisted Village*.

The foundation stone of Stisted Hall was laid by Onley-Savill-Onley on 27 September 1823, and was completed in 1825. The architect was Henry Hakewell. It replaced the old hall built by Thomas Wiseman 280 years earlier. During the Second World War the Hall was taken over by the army, and afterwards was bought by Essex County Council for use an old people's home. An eighteen-hole golf course belonging to the Braintree Golf Club now virtually surrounds the Hall.

The mews, at the east of the Hall, contained the domestic offices and the stables.

South view of the Hall showing the former rose garden.

The card above, postmarked 1908, shows one of the four fish ponds belonging to the old Hall, which it is said was a favourite retreat for the monks of Christ Church, Canterbury. The ponds were kept well stocked for the monks' support. This pond had recently been restored to its former state, although minus the railings.

"ALL SAINTS" STISTED.

BAKERS SERIES No 2.

On the south wall of All Saints' Church hangs a copy of Reubens' The Adoration of the Magi, which was painted by one of his pupils, Gaspar de Cryer, and was given to the church by Mrs Andrew Motion, whilst in residence at the Hall. The small building to the right was the village school, or Stisted Academy in the late 1830s, where pupils were taught by the Onley daughters, for 1 penny per week.

The Street taken from near the church and looking back towards the institute in about 1912, showing fine examples of the ornamental chimneys and bargeboards on the houses built by Thomas Watts of Norwich, who came to Stisted in the 1830's and worked extensively for Onley Savill Onley. Thomas Watts is buried in the churchyard and his tombstone is decorated with small replicas of his chimneys. The Stores and Post Office run by A. Baker also published postcards of the village, some of which are reproduced here.

The Street looking toward the church, with the Red Lion public house on the left. Whilst being converted to a private residence, now known as 'Rufus Leo', the skeleton of a girl was found bricked-up in a chimney. The postmark on this card is 1911.

he Stone Cottages were originally built as almshouses, and were the first houses in the llage to receive water from the reservoir built by Montefiore. Postmarked 1969 and sent to ournemouth, the writer of this postcard states 'Having a lovely break here in the real country'.

The Montefiore Institute was originally a public house the 'Duke's Head'. It was converted to a Working Men's Club/Reading Room when the Onley family took over the Hall. After Montefiore bought the Hall in 1906, he built a covered reservoir, near the village hall, and had water pumped to stand-pipes, and installed a bath-house at the institute, where, on Friday nights and Saturday afternoons, the people of Stisted could bathe for 1 penny. The Institute was given to the people of Stisted in 1916 when Mr Sebag-Montefiore sold the estate. The date of the postmark is 1920.

680. Onley Arms, Stisted.

The 'Onley Arms' stands on the site of the 'Black Lion', and was built and re-named when the Onleys took over the hall. The first landlord was Mr Albert Earle, who lived there for thirty years, and also ran the forge. The village cricket pitch was situated behind the 'Onley Arms'.

The village school, the building with the bell tower, was built in 1873 by Mr Savill Onley and bears a tablet with this date and the initials O.S.O. and J.S.O., the latter probably standing for Jane, his second wife. The first headmaster was William Rutherford, who stayed until 1885. The school was enlarged in 1963. In 1912, a group of school children visited London Zoo, an excursion paid for by Cecil Sebag-Montefiore, who at that time was a Governor of he Zoological Gardens.

The handsome house on the left of this card was the schoolmaster's house.

Gowers Farm was built in 1820. It was purchased by William McMillan in 1932 (his son still resides there) from the May family, one of whom, Francis May, introduced the first Fresian cattle to this part of Essex. Malt was made at the farm maltings and taken by road to Maldon and Heybridge. The farm stands on a drovers road from Bury St. Edmunds to Chelmsford, and then London. It was also thought to be part of a ring, starting and ending at Glastonbury, travelled by gypsies working where they could and horse-trading.

Bay Tree Farm, Stisted
A.D. 1525.

Built in 1525, the west part of Bay Tree Farm was added in the early seventeenth century.